Contents

1 THE STORY OF ELIZABETH

A portrait of the red-headed Elizabeth as the young queen.

Early life

Tudor is the surname of an English royal family, founded by a Welshman, Owen Tudor. Altogether, there were five Tudor monarchs. Here are their names, with the dates of their reigns in brackets: Henry VII (1485-1509); Henry VIII (1509-1547); Edward VI (1547-1553); Mary (1553-1558); and Elizabeth I (1558-1603).

Henry VIII had three children: Edward, Mary and Elizabeth. All of them wore the English crown. It was not always certain that Elizabeth would become queen, but the early deaths of her half-brother and half-sister left her the throne, a position that she occupied for forty-five years, until her death in 1603 at the ripe old age of 69.

Elizabeth was lucky to have survived long enough to become queen. Her early life was spent under the shadow of the axe. When her mother, Anne Boleyn, was executed, she too fell out of favour. She had to use all her native wit and intelligence to keep her head above water — and on her shoulders.

During the reigns of Elizabeth's father and brother, a change in the religion of England took place. This was called the Reformation (see page 22), and meant that England became a Protestant country and rejected the religion of the pope — Catholicism. When Queen Mary came to the throne however, she was determined to restore the Catholic religion. Unwittingly, Elizabeth became the centre of Protestant plots to overthrow the Catholic queen. There is no evidence that she supported any of these plots. Nevertheless, when Sir Thomas Wyatt rebelled against Queen Mary, Elizabeth was accused of being involved and was imprisoned in the Tower of London. There she spent her time studying. For her daily

exercise she walked along the battlement walls and looked down on the courtyard where her mother had been beheaded.

All these experiences shaped her character. Elizabeth's difficult childhood made her cunning. She combined this with a great intelligence to become one of the most successful monarchs ever to sit on the English throne.

Princess Elizabeth walks along the battlement walls of the Tower of London where she was imprisoned.

A medallion to commemorate Elizabeth's coronation.

The young queen

The English people shed few tears when Mary died in 1558. They welcomed Elizabeth to the throne because she was a Protestant and had a reputation for courage. Some people were worried that a woman would be unable to cope with the many problems that faced England at this difficult time. Apart from a tricky period in the 1650s, she proved most doubters wrong.

Elizabeth's coronation was a magnificent spectacle. The new queen was tall and slim, with a shock of fiery red hair. She had the bearing of a queen and was able to win popular support by governing with a mixture of firmness and flexibility.

There was one thing that puzzled Elizabeth's subjects. Why did she refuse to marry? She could have married anyone — and yet she never did. People were terrified that she would die without leaving a son and heir. Many bloody wars had been fought in the past because it had not been clear who should succeed to the throne. People wanted to avoid this happening again.

Elizabeth would not hear of marriage. She kept a number of suitors dangling on a string. At one time it looked likely that she would marry her favourite, Robert Dudley, the Earl of Leicester, but this never happened.

She had definite reasons for not marrying. She wanted to govern without interference from a husband, saying, 'I will have but one mistress and no master!' She also saw that it might spoil the special relationship that she had with the English people. She claimed that she was married to the kingdom of England and all her subjects were her children.

Right *Londoners crowd the streets to cheer their queen on her way to her coronation.*

The later years

As the years slipped by, Elizabeth's good looks faded and her temper grew shorter, but she lost little of her dignity and authority. 'I know I have the body of a weak and feeble woman,' she told her troops at Tilbury who were preparing to fight the Spanish Armada, 'but I have the heart and stomach of a king.'

On another occasion she hinted at the secret of her success. 'Though God has raised me high, yet I count the glory of my crown that I have reigned with your loves.'

Not everyone agreed with her, and the last years of her reign saw some troubled times. Taxes were high, vagabondage was on the increase, Spain was a constant threat, and one of her favourites rebelled against her. Yet even her critics admitted that Elizabeth was a great woman.

A story goes that a certain John Stubbs had published a complaint against the queen. He had his right hand cut off for his impertinence. After the dreadful punishment was over, he raised his hat with his left hand and cried, 'God save the Queen!'

Her reign was a time of great contrasts — of adventure and discovery, success at war, splendour at court, great theatre and poetry. For thousands of ordinary people, however, life was a hard slog. Elizabeth tried to care for all her subjects, but many went hungry, lived in hovels and could not find work. It was a glorious time for England, but not for all English people, as we shall see.

Above *The south bank of the River Thames showing the Bear Garden and the Globe theatre.*

Left *Queen Elizabeth gives her famous speech to the troops at Tilbury as they prepare to fight the Spanish.*

9

2 HOW ENGLAND WAS GOVERNED

Queen and Parliament

Queen Elizabeth addressing her most important citizens in Parliament.

When it was known that the queen was dying, Robert Cecil, her principal minister, urged her to go to bed and rest with the words: 'Madame, you must go to bed!'

'Little man! Little man!' she retorted, 'Must! Must is not (a word) allowed to be used to Princes!'

This episode shows that the queen believed that she was the boss. She alone was in charge of the affairs of her country. Although she might listen to advice, she was not forced to act upon it.

Elizabeth sat at the top of a pyramid of power. Below her was the Privy Council, a small group of advisers that met regularly with her to discuss the affairs of the realm. It included Robert Cecil's father William (Lord Burghley) and Sir Francis Walsingham who both served the queen loyally all their lives. After consulting the Privy Council, Elizabeth would decide what had to be done.

Occasionally she would call Parliament to let its members — the most wealthy and influential men in the kingdom — know what she was intending to do. The idea was growing that the monarch needed help and guidance to make sure that she acted in the interests of all English people. Elizabeth did not always have an easy time with Parliament. They could be argumentative, but they were always loyal. Parliament even imprisoned one of its

Right *Queen Elizabeth liked to show herself to her people as often as possible. Here she is being carried through the crowds who are desperate to catch a glimpse of their queen.*

10

members — Peter Wentworth — for being critical of the queen.

The key to her success was that most English people agreed with Elizabeth about what was best for their country.

Local government

Above *A Justice of the Peace checks the quality of beer in a country inn.*

It is no good making a law unless there are people all over the country who see that it is obeyed. To allow this to happen, the Tudors created a system of local government. This meant that there were officials throughout England who tried to make sure that what the queen wanted to take place, actually happened.

Communications were bad. There were no national newspapers, no radio and no television. In those parts of the country furthest from the influence of the capital, London, there were councils who had to keep law and order in their areas. The 'Council of the North' was in charge of the country north of the River Trent. The 'Council of the Marches' cared for the troublesome border country between England and Wales.

Away from those areas, the country was divided up into counties. In charge of each county was a lord-lieutenant,

A pewter tankard used during Elizabeth's reign.

chosen by the queen. He had a team of men working for him. At the local level, the most important of these officials were the Justices of the Peace (J.P.s) who were the 'eyes and ears of the Crown'.

Sir Nathaniel Bacon was one such J.P. He lived in Norfolk and came from a well-to-do family. His work as a J.P. was varied and time-consuming. He had to deal with the punishment of criminals, witches and rogues. He had to check inns to make sure that the beer was good. He collected taxes, supervised the Poor Law (see page 42), and made sure that his area contributed enough men, money and equipment in times of war.

The system seemed to work efficiently and continued to do so as long as the outlying counties had faith in their monarch. Elizabeth had such command over the loyalty of her subjects that this trust was seldom in doubt.

3 THREATS AT HOME

Mary, Queen of Scots.

Mary Queen of Scots

It would be wrong to pretend that there was no opposition to Elizabeth within England itself. The biggest threat to the queen came from her cousin, Mary, Queen of Scots, and from Mary's Catholic supporters.

Mary had an extraordinary life. It started with great promise and ended in tragedy. She became Queen of Scotland when she was less than a week old, and, on her marriage to Francis II, Queen of France as well when she was still a teenager. Added to this, many people believed that she — and not Elizabeth — was the rightful Queen of England.

Things started to go wrong when she returned to Scotland and became involved in murder and intrigue. Her second husband, the unpleasant Lord Darnley, was murdered on the orders of the Earl of Bothwell who became Mary's third husband only three months after Darnley's brutal murder. As it was obvious that Mary had something to do with the killing, the Scottish people rebelled against her. She fought and lost the Battle of

Left *Catholics plot to overthrow Elizabeth and put Mary on the throne.*

Langdale, and fled to England to seek Elizabeth's protection.

Mary's presence in England was awkward for Elizabeth. She immediately became the focus of Catholic plots to overthrow Elizabeth. Anti-Catholic feeling was strong but for almost nineteen years, Elizabeth ignored the advice of her councillors that Mary was dangerous and should be put to death.

Finally she became convinced by evidence from her spies that Mary was actively plotting with Catholics to overthrow her. Even so, it was with great reluctance that she ordered Mary's execution. Her command was carried out in the Great Hall of Fotheringay Castle on 8th February 1587.

Mary, Queen of Scots goes bravely to her death.

The Earl of Essex

Robert Devereux, the Earl of Essex.

Robert Devereux, the second Earl of Essex, was a handsome, proud and ambitious man. He soon became a favourite of the ageing queen because of his good looks and charm.

At court, Elizabeth was in a position to give favours. Those courtiers who received her favours could become rich and powerful men. This system of patronage, as it was called, was a way of buying support. It had worked well for most of the reign.

Unfortunately, after Lord Burghley's death in 1598, two rival groups emerged. One was led by Robert Cecil, Burghley's son, the other by the dashing and headstrong Earl of Essex. There was not room for both of them at court. Although Elizabeth loved Essex, she was not prepared to give important posts to his supporters. He could be very rude to her and once Elizabeth boxed his ears in public.

In 1599, Elizabeth decided to send him to crush a rebellion in Ireland, to get him out of the way. After six months of useless fighting, Essex returned to England without being asked to do so. He knew that the longer he was away from the court, the more powerful his enemy, Cecil, would become. The queen was furious that he had disobeyed orders. He was arrested. His days of greatness were numbered.

In a foolish attempt to revenge his fall from power, he planned an uprising to 'save the queen from her wicked advisers'. In February 1600, he rode through London with 200 armed men, a group of misfits who had a grudge against Cecil. The Londoners ignored him and the rebellion fizzled out. Essex was convicted of high treason and executed on 25th February 1601. For months afterwards, the queen wept for the death of her wayward favourite.

An Elizabethan soldier.

Below *Poorly-armed Irish soldiers prepare to attack a column of English troops led by the Earl of Essex.*

4 THREATS FROM ABROAD

Piracy and the power of Spain

'It is easier to find flocks of white crows than one Englishman who loves a foreigner', a historian once wrote. Englishmen disliked all foreigners, but especially the Spanish. Spain in those days was the wealthiest and most

powerful country in the world. England was jealous of her riches, and there were many other reasons why the two countries became such bitter enemies.

Spain was the pioneer of exploration in the New World across the Atlantic Ocean, and had carved out a great empire in South and Central America. No one was allowed to trade with her colonies, which infuriated the English merchants and seamen. A band of English sea dogs decided to take the law into their own hands.

Sir John Hawkins, a young sea captain, started an illegal trade in slaves. He bought them in Africa, and sailed across to Central America where he sold them to the Spanish landowners at a huge profit. On his third expedition, he was trapped in the Mexican port of San Juan de Ulua. The Spaniards swore to let him and his men go free, but broke their promise. They opened fire, and only two ships escaped. Aboard one of them was Francis Drake, a fiery young adventurer.

Drake swore to pay the Spaniards back for their treachery. For the next twenty years (1567-1587), he waged a private war against Spain. He plundered Spanish settlements in America, and captured Spanish ships which were overflowing with treasure.

King Philip II of Spain was infuriated by these acts of piracy. He was sure that Drake's ships were gifts from Elizabeth, the 'heretic' queen. He determined to teach her a lesson that neither she nor her people would ever forget. Plans went rapidly ahead to invade England and return it to the true faith — Catholicism.

An Elizabethan sailor.

Left *A battle rages in the Mexican port of San Juan de Ulua between the Spaniards and a force of English sea dogs led by Sir John Hawkins.*

The Spanish Armada

In 1588, Drake was enjoying a quiet game of bowls in Plymouth when a frantic sea captain interrupted him with the news that the Spanish Armada had been sighted in the English Channel. He made the famous reply 'We have time to finish the game, and beat the Spaniards too!'

The Spanish plan was to send their Armada of 130 ships to defeat the English fleet at sea. It would then link up with a massive army waiting in the Netherlands, and escort it over to England where Spain assumed her troops would be victorious.

The plan misfired for a number of reasons. The English were better sailors. Their ships were slightly smaller, could sail faster, and had heavier firepower. The Spanish fleet was an army afloat. They were unable to get close enough to the English ships to board them and so benefit from their greater size. The English also had better leaders. Lord Howard of Effingham and Sir Francis Drake were excellent commanders. The Spanish leader was the Duke of Medina Sidonia. He was seasick as soon as his flagship put to sea. He was no match for his English rivals.

The skills of the English fleet were shown as they chased the Armada down the Channel, sinking or capturing any galleon that came adrift from the pack. Yet the Armada still remained intact. Almost in desperation the English sent fire ships into the massed Spanish fleet as they lay at anchor off Calais. Panic ensued, the Armada split up and fled north. They met terrible storms. Many were shipwrecked on the west coast of Ireland. Weeks later, the survivors — less than half the original fleet — limped home. The Spanish army in the Netherlands was never used. The Armada had failed.

Right *A Spanish galleon explodes after suffering a direct hit during the fierce fighting in the English Channel.*

Above *A medal struck in 1588 to celebrate England's victory over the Spanish Armada.*

5 RELIGION

The Reformation

The Tudor period up to Elizabeth's accession was a time of great religious turmoil. The Catholic Church claimed to be the 'One True Church'. At its head was the pope, the 'Vicar of Christ', who lived in Rome. In Europe a man called Martin Luther (1483-1546) challenged the pope's authority. He disagreed with many things the Catholic Church said and found that he had many supporters. This break with the pope was called the Reformation. The new faith was called Protestantism.

In Henry VIII's reign, these ideas filtered across the Channel to England. He used them because they suited his selfish purposes. He wanted to annul his marriage to Catherine of Aragon because she had not produced a son and heir to the throne. The pope refused, so Henry took matters into his own hands. He proclaimed himself — and not the pope — the head of the English Church. The marriage was dissolved.

Henry VIII also needed money, so he ordered that the monasteries be destroyed. Many of them were fabulously wealthy. Their riches went to the Crown. Few people objected — some remained loyal to the pope, but most English people were happy to break with Rome.

In Edward VI's reign, anti-Catholic feeling continued and the Protestant Church grew in strength. Queen Mary was a devout Catholic and she tried to reverse this process. She ordered that 300 Protestants be burnt at the stake, including Archbishop Cranmer; renewed links with the pope; and married King Philip II of Spain, a leading Catholic. She soon found that she was swimming against the tide, and died a desperately unhappy woman.

22

Elizabeth's answer

When Elizabeth came to the throne, the Protestants breathed a great sigh of relief. Elizabeth wanted to please them. She also wanted to keep the Catholics happy. Her chief concern was to make sure that her subjects were loyal to her. She knew that if they were content, they would be less likely to rebel. So she tried to steer a middle course between the extreme Protestantism of Edward VI's reign, and Mary's rigid Catholicism.

Sometimes it is hard for us to imagine what all the fuss was about. As long as you believed in the Christian God, what did it matter whether you called yourself a Catholic or a Protestant?

Protestants asked themselves important questions. How can we make sure that we go to Heaven and not burn in the fires of hell forever? Is there any human being who can really speak for God? Who should be the head of the

Queen Mary I

24

Above *A Puritan prayer meeting.*

Church? Is it right that the Church should have so much money? Should priests be allowed to marry? They came up with very different answers to the ones the Catholic Church had given for centuries.

Both sides believed that they were right. If they were right, then the other 'side' must be wrong and must be punished until they changed their minds and saw the truth.

The answers Elizabeth gave to these questions allowed Catholics a certain amount of freedom. They also pleased most Protestants — but not all. There was a group of people who believed that Elizabeth had not gone nearly far enough to stamp out all traces of Catholicism. This group was growing in power and importance. They were called the Puritans. They were to play an important part in the history of the next hundred years.

A witch in a ducking-stool about to be submerged in a river.

Witchcraft

Religion played a big part in everyone's life, from the richest person to the poorest. No one doubted that God existed. The church (along with the manor house and the village) was the centre of people's lives. A law said that everyone over six had to go to church on Sundays. If they did not, they had to pay a fine.

It was a difficult law to enforce and priests moaned that people preferred to go to markets and fairs on Sundays. The churches were cold and damp and the services long and often dismal, so perhaps you couldn't blame them.

This did not stop them from believing in God. They also believed in the devil just as much. They feared that if they did not lead good lives they would burn forever in the fires of hell. They were very superstitious too. If anything went wrong with their lives and they could not explain it, they searched for a scapegoat.

Witches were blamed for ruined harvests and other accidents. Shakespeare wrote about some witches in his play *Macbeth*. They are typical of what people believed witches to look like. They were usually haggard old women casting evil spells over a bubbling cauldron:

'. . . *For a charm of powerful trouble,*
Like a hell-broth, boil and bubble.'

In Europe, thousands of witches were tortured and killed by the Inquisition. In England, only a few witches were killed, but many were pilloried or put in ducking-stools. It was a long time before people realized that there were no such things as witches — or are there?

Right *Hag-like witches cast a spell to call up demons to carry out their evil wishes.*

6 EVERYDAY LIFE

Life at court

The queen's court was one of the most magnificent in all Europe. It was the place where young men and women gathered to 'pay court' to their queen, hoping to impress her. Wherever Elizabeth stayed — in Whitehall Palace, Greenwich Palace, or in other stately homes throughout the country — a troupe of courtiers, ladies-in-waiting and hangers-on would follow.

For most of the day, the queen would work quietly in the Privy Chamber on affairs of State. In the evenings or at weekends, Elizabeth held audiences when courtiers could speak to her and suggest ideas which they hoped would meet with royal approval. A favourable word from the queen could make you rich and famous.

A 'miniature' painting by Nicholas Hilliard of an Elizabethan courtier.

Right *Queen Elizabeth dances the 'Galliard' with one of her courtiers.*

There were other ways to impress the queen. The Elizabethan court was the scene of lively entertainments — music, dancing, and the clowning of Richard Tarleton, the court jester. The young courtiers spent a fortune on their clothes. They strutted around in their jewel-studded doublets and breeches like splendid peacocks, trying to catch the eye of the queen. Only a few succeeded in winning her favour.

In the summer months, the queen and her court travelled around the country on magnificent royal 'progresses'. Wherever she went, crowds lined the roads, cheering their queen.

Many courtiers found the court a 'glittering misery'. They paid out a lot of money — and got nowhere. However, it served the queen well. It meant that she could reward loyalty and impress visiting royalty with the splendour of her Majesty.

Life in London

A view of London and the River Thames.

In a rage, Queen Mary I had once threatened to take her court away from London. The unspoken answer of Londoners had been, 'Fine. Take your court, but leave us the River Thames.' The Thames was the main artery of the kingdom, its lifeline with Europe and the outside world. It brought trade and wealth into England. On its banks, like a leech sucking up its riches, prospered the city of London.

Already, London was the third biggest city in the western world — after Naples and Constantinople. It was the political, judicial and financial centre of the land. Some 200,000 people lived there and the number was growing all the time.

London was a city of contrasts. It was an exciting but risky place. A city of whirlwind activity — for those lucky enough to have a job. It was beautiful in parts — and squalid in others. It was a city filled with palaces, rich merchant's houses, the shops and halls of the Master Guilds — and hovels too. The queen lived near London. Her poorest citizens lived within its walls.

London had wonderful things to look at — London Bridge spanning the river; and horrific things to see — the heads of executed men decaying on Traitor's Gate. It was a place of opportunity — and disease. What you could not escape from was the stench of the open drains and rotting garbage. Or the deafening sounds that echoed down the narrow streets — the crashing of cartwheels on the cobbles, the clanging bells of the numerous churches, the shouts of hawkers selling their wares, or the watermen calling you to take their boat up or down the river.

At ease in the country

By the time of Elizabeth's death, there were almost five million people in England. Nine out of every ten lived in the country. Although only a few of them were rich, this minority owned most of the land in England. They built themselves magnificent houses. Some, such as Longleat and Montacute House, still stand today.

These country houses — made from timber or stone — were designed to be comfortable dwelling-places. The peace of Elizabeth's reign meant that great landlords no longer had to wall themselves up in draughty fortresses. They could concentrate on comfort and fine living. Their houses had large glass windows to let the sunlight in, and were topped with a maze of chimneys to allow the smoke to escape from the large fireplaces.

Montacute House in Somerset, built in 1600.

While the master of the house was away — either at court or looking after his farm — his wife was in charge of keeping a well-run house. She and her staff of butlers, cooks and maids had to make candles, brew beer, collect firewood, and provide food. This last task alone kept her very busy. When a lord and his lady once entertained the queen and her court, they got through three oxen and 140 geese for breakfast!

Despite a full day, there was always time for fun. The rich pursued the age-old sports of hunting and falconry, and showed an interest in some new games, such as 'real' tennis. In the evenings, they entertained their guests with music and dancing.

These mansions were often far away from towns and could only be reached along dreadful roads. The people who lived in them had to be self-sufficient — to provide the things they needed for themselves.

A nobleman discusses building plans for his house with the architect.

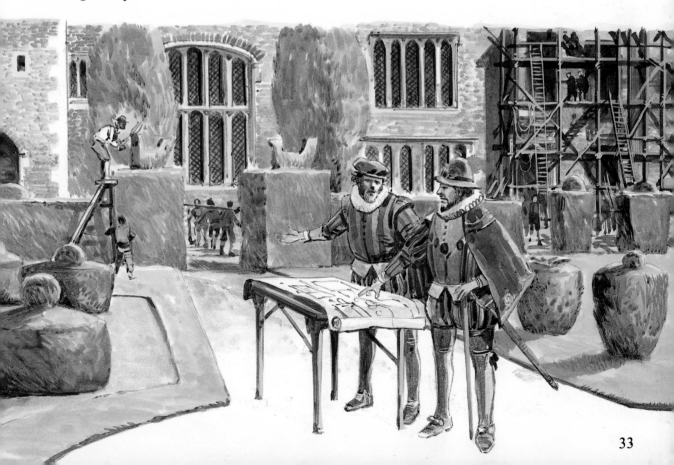

33

Merchants and traders

If it had been possible to fly over England in Elizabeth's day, you would have noticed that much of the country was covered in forest. Dotted about were villages, surrounded by strips of cultivated land and joined by twisting cart tracks. Occasionally, you would have spotted small towns, usually close to the sea.

London was by far the biggest city, but even though it was spreading beyond its medieval walls, it was an easy walk from anywhere in the city into the countryside. No other English town had more than 20,000 inhabitants. Towns like Norwich, Exeter and York had grown up because they were well placed for commerce and industry.

People were rich in the country if they owned land. In towns, money was to be made in business. During Elizabeth's reign England became one of the top trading nations and her merchants became very wealthy. They were often to be seen in their fine clothes down by the docks, welcoming a valuable cargo of wine, silk and spices from abroad. Their profits came from buying these goods cheaply and selling them at a higher price. Such men belonged to one of the important livery companies — the Drapers and the Goldsmiths for example — which had great influence within the towns.

If they were successful, these men built smart town houses and lived very well. Like their country counterparts, they too had time for fun. In London they could watch one of Shakespeare's plays at the Globe, gamble on the cockfights in Drury Lane, practise their archery in Moorfields, or enjoy the latest craze, smoking tobacco. Although they owed their riches to what towns could offer, most of these men had one ambition — to buy land and build a house in the country.

A wealthy London merchant.

Opposite *A bustling scene in London's busy docks.*

The poor in the country

Life for the poor was not so enjoyable. Most of them lived in one-room, mud-floored dwellings that they shared with their animals, and worked on the land as agricultural labourers. A handful owned a few fields, but mostly they rented their land off a big landowner or smaller farmer. Some worked on the noble's estate itself.

They sweated away from dawn to dusk, often seven days a week, on the grinding routine of ploughing, harrowing, sowing, reaping and harvesting the crops. They worked to survive, to provide enough food for their families.

Elizabethan writers believed that there was something romantic about the lives of these hardy labourers, particularly the shepherd and the blacksmith. In fact, they had a tougher time during Elizabeth's reign than before. The population was growing which led to worse poverty

A boy's leather jerkin.

Farm workers burn the
hedgerows that landowners put
up to 'enclose' their fields.

because there were more mouths to feed. Also, rich
farmers started to 'enclose' their fields and rear sheep on
them where before people had been growing crops and
vegetables. The result was unemployment and hunger
among the poorest people.

On rare occasions there was something to break up the
dull and back-breaking pattern of life. There were
Christian festivals to celebrate, and pagan rituals, like the
crowning of the Lord of Misrule, to enjoy. Actors,
minstrels and jugglers travelled around the country per-
forming to enthusiastic audiences.

The main 'sport' was poaching, to add some meat to
their diet. Occasionally, the men played a violent game
similar to football, or sat on river banks and fished for
their supper. The greatest escape was the ale house where
they often drank themselves into a stupor to forget the
drudgery of their working lives.

The poor in the towns

Those people who were unable to find work in the country, drifted into the towns where there was a greater variety of work on offer. The fortunate ones found employment of one sort or another.

A typical market scene at Cheapside in London would be full of such characters. Porters groaning under heavy loads, drivers of carts whipping their horses through the narrow streets, stall-holders calling out their bargains, coal-black chimney sweeps looking for another chimney to clean, bearwards showing off their pet bears, and servants buying food for their rich masters. Down by the river, dock workers toiled to bring cargoes ashore and wherrymen ferried wealthy passengers over the water.

A woman sells apples on the crowded streets of London.

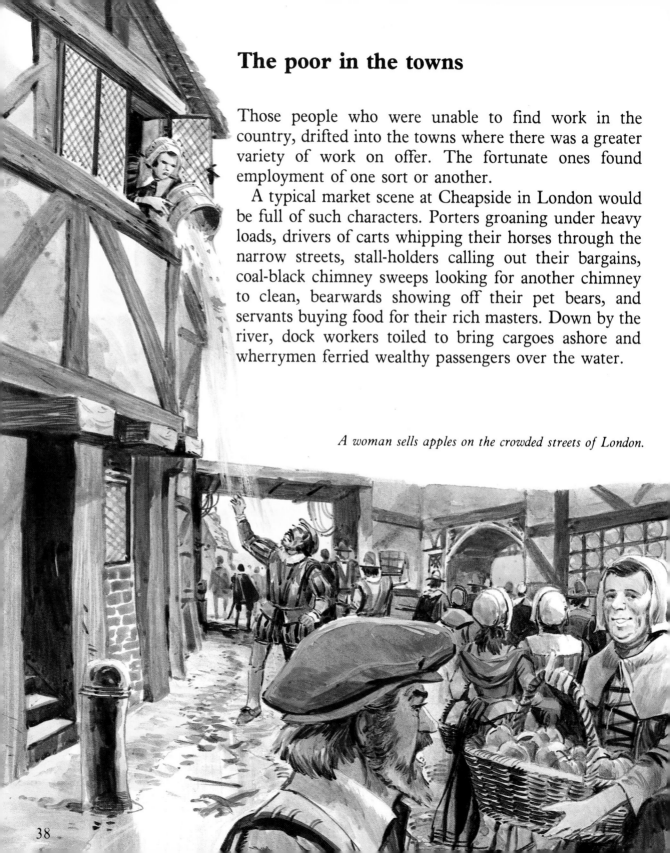

The very lucky ones managed to become apprentices in one of the Master Trades. At the end of a long seven-year apprenticeship, they became craftsmen and could set up their own business in printing, shoe-making, or whatever. The apprentices had a reputation for being riotous. A law was passed in 1588 to try and make them wear less outrageous clothes and behave better. It did not have much effect!

For light relief, the poor people in the towns watched the bloodthirsty sports of cockfighting and bear-baiting or, as in 1581, went to Fleet Street to see human 'wonders of the world' — a huge giant and a tiny dwarf — on display.

There were some people who were too poor even to enjoy this entertainment. Their dream of living in a town had become a nightmare. Unable to find work, they turned to crime as the only way to make ends meet. They lived in squalid, rat-infested slums and must have had miserable lives. They had no share in the glories of Elizabeth's reign.

Two rubbish collectors try to keep the streets clean.

Education

It is sometimes said that your schooldays are the best days of your life. Although you may not agree, one thing is certain — education today is far more lively and varied than it was for Tudor children. Their workload was hard, the hours long and the discipline tough.

Their schoolday began at 6 a.m. in the summer, and 7 a.m. in the winter. Apart from a break for lunch and fifteen minutes off for breakfast, it was all work and no play until they finished at 5.30 p.m. This gruelling programme started when you were only five or six years old and could last for ten years with only short holidays to break up the routine.

In the poorly-lit and heavily-timbered classrooms, children were fed an unappetizing diet of Latin, more Latin, Greek, 'grammar' and religious knowledge. Using goose quills which splodged ink everywhere, they were required to write out chunks of *Aesop's Fables* or Caesar's *Gallic Wars* — and then learn them by heart.

A child practises reading to his teacher.

The idea was that information should be drummed into you. If you failed to take it in, the teacher thrashed you with a birch rod. They always had a bundle of canes close at hand — and used them freely. Not everyone went to school. Girls and children from poor families often went without education, and so had little chance of improving themselves.

If all this sounds grim, things were in fact getting better. During Elizabeth's reign, many famous public and grammar schools were founded; printed school textbooks were far more widely used; and the system did produce some remarkable and cultured people (see page 48).

A Tudor classroom scene showing the results of bad work.

Poverty and the Poor Law

'Hark! Hark! The dogs do bark. The beggars are coming to town.' So chanted the townspeople as hordes of vagabonds invaded their towns, their bodies covered in sores and dressed in rags. These vagabonds were poor people — without money, a home or a future. Their numbers were increasing all the time.

During Elizabeth's reign, prices of food and goods rocketed, but pay did not. There was also high unemployment with thousands thrown out of work by the policy of enclosure (see page 37). Many tramped the roads searching for a living — and were forced to beg to keep themselves alive.

Below *A band of hungry vagabonds cause havoc in a peaceful market town.*

What did Elizabeth do about the poor and the homeless? The monasteries had looked after the poor and now they were gone. Her answer was to pass some laws aimed to help the poor.

The most famous of these Poor Laws started to work in 1601. It was harsh towards those who were poor but also physically fit. They could be whipped, branded or even executed if they carried on begging. Towards those too weak to work, the law was more caring. The rich people of each parish were forced to pay some money which was used to build shelters for the poor.

A rich man gives money to a beggar.

Unfortunately, most Tudors believed that poverty was a punishment from God. Others thought that beggars were just lazy. They were not willing to help, and therefore many people stayed poor and hungry. Without the Poor Laws, they would have been even worse off.

Crime and punishment

The Tudors had a simple and harsh attitude towards crime. If you were caught committing a serious crime, you might hang for it, or spend a lifetime in prison. But, despite brutal punishments, crime was common.

In towns, you had to watch out — there was a coney-catcher about! This would be a man or woman who tried to get you to part with your money either by tricking you into giving it to them, or by stealing it. Many wealthy visitors to the crowded market-places would discover their money had been stolen by a pickpocket or a cutpurse. Sometimes the thieves worked in gangs, like in Dickens' *Oliver Twist*, 300 years later.

There were other types of criminals too. On moonlit nights, highwaymen held up travellers by deserted road-sides; horse-thieves raided stables on lonely country estates; 'anglers' stole richly-embroidered clothes from washing lines using a long pole; and 'moonmen' asked farmers for shelter — and then stole their poultry in the middle of the night. Of the more serious crimes, murder seemed to be more a habit of the rich and powerful people in the country, and so they often got away with it.

One of the reasons that criminals took the risk of being caught was that they seldom were. There was no organized police force and no effective methods of detection. Law enforcement was the job of the parish constable. He

Left *A cut-purse wearing a large cloak to hide the bag of money that he has stolen from a wealthy man.*

44

and his dog wandered around the streets keeping an eye open for trouble-makers and calling out the hour: 'Twelve of the clock, look well to your locks.' If trouble did break out, what could one man do on his own?

Criminals often got away with their crimes, but not always. An Essex woman, Agnes Osier, stole two sheets and sixty shillings and hanged for it. Then, as now, crime was not worth the risk.

Above *Petty criminals were punished by being put in stocks like these.*

Below *An able-bodied vagabond is tied to a stake waiting to be branded with a red-hot iron.*

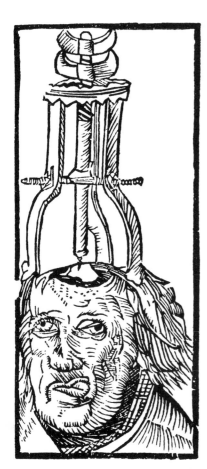

Above A trepanning operation to raise a crushed skull.

Health and medicine

In Tudor times there was no National Health Service, no preventive medicine, no anaesthetics and no vaccines. People had only the vaguest idea of how the body worked and so most bodies went unmended.

The general state of health was very poor. Most children died before the age of five. Only one in ten reached old age — 40 years old. Queen Elizabeth lived to be 69 which was very old in those days. She nearly fell victim to smallpox when she was only 29. Although she survived, she bore the ugly scars of the disease to her grave.

Lack of hygiene helped spread disease. Poor sanitation created a breeding ground for germs. The Tudors had no

Right *A man grits his teeth as his leg is amputated without anaesthetic.*

barriers against these germs, and once their bodies were infected they could do little to make themselves healthy once more.

Most people prayed that the illness should leave them — but their prayers were seldom answered. The popular practice of blood-letting was of no use. Some tried horrific rituals. For example, victims of epilepsy drank water from the skull of a murdered person — and died just the same.

Others used herbal remedies, but these rarely worked. Limbs that had gone rotten were brutally amputated with a saw and without anaesthetic. Teeth were extracted with no injection to relieve the pain.

There were few skilful doctors, surgeons or dentists. Some individuals tried hard to improve medical knowledge and practice, but progress was slow. Death from disease was always just around the corner and Tudor people always lived in its shadow.

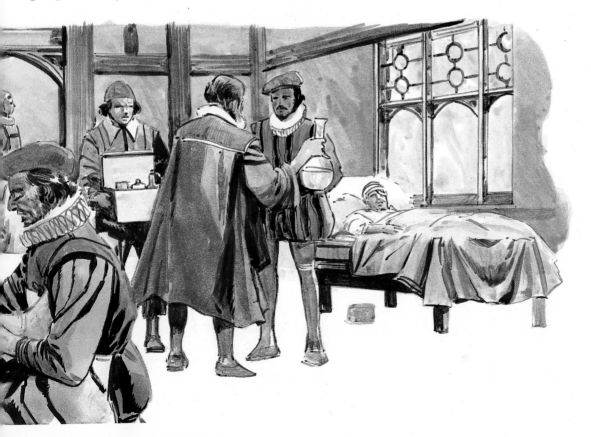

Above *William Shakespeare, the famous playwright.*

Arts and the theatre

Elizabeth's reign saw a phenomenal rise in the popularity of the theatre. Tudor people had a great sense of fun and loved to watch plays so they could forget about the harshness of their lives. Travelling players still toured the country as they had done for centuries, but under Elizabeth, three permanent theatres were built in London.

The most famous of these was the Globe. It was here that the plays of William Shakespeare — perhaps the best known Englishman of all time — and Christopher Marlowe, killed in a pub brawl, were first performed.

Today, there is usually a hushed silence in theatres. In those days, audiences could be incredibly rowdy. The 'groundlings' — those who paid a penny to get in — crowded around the stage. They jeered and cheered, cracked nutshells under their feet and slurped on steaming bowls of soup. If they did not like the villain of the plot, they would hurl rotten vegetables at the unfortunate actor.

However, just as often they could be spellbound by the beautiful costumes, the fine speeches and the goriness of the death scenes when guts from the local butchers were splashed across the stage. Not everyone enjoyed the fun though. Many Puritans in London frowned on the riotous goings-on. The Corporation even closed down one of the theatres — a foretaste of things to come.

Other arts flourished too. The period is remembered for the delicate miniature portraits of Nicholas Hilliard; the poetry of Sir Philip Sidney, so tragically killed in battle; and the music of Tallis and Byrd. Culturally, it was a period of almost unequalled richness and creativity.

Above *The Globe theatre.*

Right *A dramatic scene from one of Shakespeare's well-known plays.*

7 VOYAGES OF DISCOVERY

Exploration and settlement

Today, it is the vastness of space that is unexplored and unknown. In those days, what happened on earth was as much of a mystery. During this period, intrepid explorers set out to solve the puzzle.

Why did sailors and merchants risk their lives on these perilous missions? Sir Walter Raleigh, a daring English explorer, gave us an answer: 'to seek new worlds, for gold, for praise, for glory'. Apart from curiosity, a more selfish reason was to find fame and fortune.

Spain and Portugal were the pioneers of exploration. Vasco da Gama, Columbus, Ferdinand Magellan and others sailed from their ports to make exciting discoveries. When the English realized that money was to be made, they organized their own expeditions.

These met with mixed fortunes. The Arctic missions of Frobisher and Chancellor failed to find a northern passage to the riches of the East. Merchants resorted to

Right *A ship in Elizabeth's navy.*

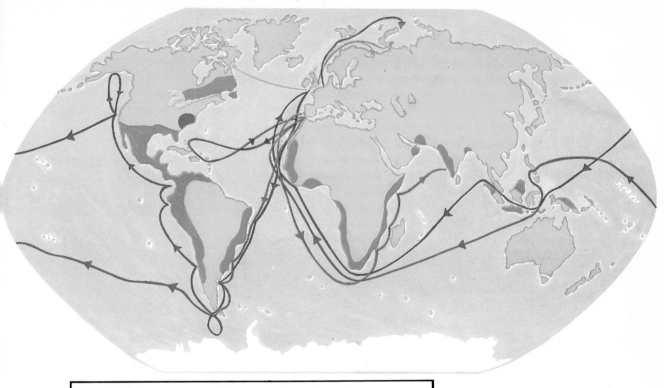

Above *A map of the world showing the major voyages of discovery in the period.*

the safer route round Africa. They founded the East India Company in 1601 which became very profitable.

The idea was growing that once a place had been explored, people should settle down to live there. England experimented with these 'colonies' and in 1584, Raleigh set up the colony of Virginia. Unfortunately, due to lack of supplies and hostile Red Indians, this community failed to take root. Within a few years however, similar colonies would be flourishing.

These voyages fired the public imagination. By the end of the Elizabethan age, the world was a smaller and more familiar place.

Below *An astrolabe used to measure the height of the stars.*

Drake's voyage round the world

The Spaniards called Francis Drake 'El Draque', which means the Dragon. They believed that he had magical powers and could see ships over the horizon. He was feared and respected by both friend and foe. Under his leadership, men were prepared to go to the ends of the earth.

In 1577, Drake set out on an expedition to plunder Spanish settlements in South America. He had no idea of where his voyage would take him, or how long it would last. In the giant seas off the southern tip of South America, one of his small fleet sank and the others returned home. By the time that the storm had blown itself out, Drake's ship, the *Golden Hind,* was alone in the Pacific.

Undaunted, Drake sailed up and down the coasts of Chile and Peru stealing treasure from the Spanish. Laden with gold and precious stones, he sailed west across the Pacific. He almost met with disaster when the *Golden Hind* ran aground on a reef in the unexplored seas north of Australia. Luckily, when they had jettisoned some of their cargo, they floated free.

The rest of their epic voyage went without a hitch. They rounded the Cape of Good Hope, at the southern tip of Africa, and returned to Plymouth in September 1580 to a heroes' welcome. They had been away almost three years.

It was an incredible feat of endurance for Drake and all his crew. Sailing in those days was tough and dangerous. The food was usually bad, the water stale, and living quarters cramped. On any long voyage, a large number of the crew died from disease. One can only admire these men as they risked their lives in search of riches and adventure.

Elizabeth

54

8 THE ELIZABETHAN AGE

Queen Elizabeth I died on 24th March 1603. Only a few months earlier, she had been riding ten miles a day. She had decided that her job was done, and life slipped away from her 'easily, like a ripe apple from a tree'. The whole nation mourned the death of their beloved queen. In a magnificent and sombre ceremony, over a thousand people walked behind her coffin to Westminster Abbey. They were watched by crowds of weeping men, women and children. Their 'good Queen Bess' was gone, never to return.

Elizabeth had been their queen for almost 45 years. She was not perfect, and is not above criticism. Elizabeth had spent most of the crown's own money so that her successor, James I, found himself poor and therefore weak. The religious differences had been shelved — not solved. Her government perhaps relied too heavily on her own skilful and strong personality for it to work efficiently. Although she cared about all her people, life for the poor remained tough.

Nevertheless, she was a remarkable queen who was widely loved and respected. One foreigner wrote, 'It is more to have seen Elizabeth than to have seen England.' Elizabeth symbolized England's new-found strength, prosperity and prestige. She had inherited a deeply-divided nation. Using a mixture of charm and firmness, she soothed the differences and brought peace to her people.

Her reign is famous for the defeat of the Armada, Drake's voyages and Shakespeare's plays. It is also a fascinating story of a relationship between a queen and her people, a 'marriage' that made England feared and envied throughout Europe.

The great events and figures of the Elizabethan Age showing Lord Burghley, Shakespeare, Mary Tudor, Raleigh, Drake, Marlowe and Elizabeth I herself.

Table of dates

1485 Henry VII, the first of the Tudors becomes king.

1492 Christopher Columbus discovers America.

1509 Henry VII dies. His son, Henry VIII, succeeds him to the throne.

1533 Henry VIII's marriage to Catherine of Aragon is declared null and void. Henry marries Ann Boleyn. Their daughter, Elizabeth, is born.

1536 Ann Boleyn is beheaded.

1536-39 Dissolution of the Monasteries.

1542 Mary, Queen of Scots, born.

1547 Henry VIII dies. His son, Edward VI, succeeds to the throne.

1553 Willoughby and Chancellor's expedition to find a north-east passage to the East.

Edward VI dies. Mary comes to the throne.

1554 Wyatt's rebellion. Elizabeth is sent to the Tower.

1558 Mary dies. Elizabeth becomes queen.

1562 Elizabeth almost dies of smallpox.

1564 William Shakespeare is born.

1566 Lord Darnley, Mary, Queen of Scots' second husband, is murdered.

1567 Spanish treachery at San Juan de Ulua, in the Caribbean.

1576 Peter Wentworth, M.P., is imprisoned by Parliament.

Frobisher's first expedition in search of a north-west passage to the East.

1577-80 Drake's voyage around the world.

1580 Longleat House completed.

1584 Colony of Virginia founded.

1586 Sir Philip Sidney killed at Battle of Zutphen in the Netherlands.

1587 Mary, Queen of Scots, executed at Fotheringay for high treason.

1588 The Spanish Armada sails against England and is defeated.

1589 Chelmsford Witch Trials.

1593 Christopher Marlowe, leading playwright, is killed in pub brawl.

1598 William Cecil (Lord Burghley), Elizabeth's leading adviser, dies.

1598-99 Globe Theatre is built.

1601 The Earl of Essex is beheaded after his abortive rebellion in 1600.

East India Company is founded.

The most important Poor Law is passed.

1603 Elizabeth I dies. James VI of Scotland becomes James I of England.

New words

Anaesthetic A drug that puts the nervous system to sleep so that operations can be carried out painlessly.

Breeches Short trousers fastened below the knee.

Colony A group of people that leave their own land, and settle in a distant and unexplored part of the world.

Court The place where the queen is staying, or the people (courtiers) who spent their lives in attendance on the queen.

Doublet A short, fashionable jacket.

Ducking-stool A stool on the end of a long pole that was balanced out over a river. For a punishment, a witch would be placed in the stool and 'ducked'.

Enclosure The policy of farmers to take over common land, put a hedge around it, and graze sheep on it.

Falconry The sport of using birds of prey to hunt for small animals like rabbits.

Guild An organization to which members of a profession or trade belonged.

Hawker Someone who sells things on the streets or in markets.

Hovel A very poor dwelling-place.

Inflation A state of the economy when prices rise very rapidly.

Inquisition The ruthless persecution and horrible torture of people who were suspected of not being true Catholics. It was carried out in Europe for centuries.

J.P. Justice of the Peace — a local government official with various duties to perform in the countryside where he lived.

Minstrel A travelling musician or singer.

Plot A plan or conspiracy that intends to drastically change the way things are.

Poaching Hunting for game on land that does not belong to you.

'Progress' A trip that Elizabeth used to make from London to visit her friends and see her subjects in the country.

Parliament A gathering of the most important people in the kingdom at Westminster to advise and assist the queen in the running of the country.

Pillory A wooden frame with holes for the head and arms. People who had misbehaved were locked into the frame which stood in a public place. They would then be ridiculed and pelted with mud etc.

Privy Council A group of advisers close to the queen who helped her in the difficult task of governing the country.

Puritans Religious people with a hatred for the pope and Catholicism.

Quill The hollow stem of a feather made into a pen and used for writing.

Real tennis A game that the Tudors played which resembled modern tennis.

Reformation A European religious movement in the sixteenth century that changed the things that it thought were wrong with the Catholic Church, and started the Reformed — or Protestant — Churches.

Scapegoat A person who is blamed for something going wrong when it is not their fault.

Sea dog An English sailor who raided Spanish shipping and Spanish land in South America.

Treason Disloyalty to the monarch.

Vaccine A substance taken to ensure that the human body does not contract certain diseases.

Further information

Places to visit

Museums Every county in Britain has dozens of museums open to the public, far too many to list here. You should be able to find something about the Tudors at your nearest one. The Museum of London has a good collection of Tudor artefacts and you can find other material in the Geffrye Museum, also in London.

Famous sites The Tudors were great builders. They constructed many fine town and country houses, many of which are still standing. Some of these, like Speke Hall near Liverpool and Hampton Court in London, are open to the public and are well worth a visit. A trip to Stratford-upon-Avon, Shakespeare's birthplace, is worthwhile too. For a fascinating insight into life in the Tudor navy, visit Henry VIII's flagship — the *Mary Rose* — in Portsmouth. It is quite likely that there are some Tudor houses in your local area. Write to the National Trust enclosing a stamped, addressed envelope for a list of Tudor sites near your home.

Libraries The local library can always give information about the best places to visit, both near your home and farther afield. Most libraries have a section on local history. Try to discover what the Tudors were up to in your area.

Books

Clarke, Amanda, *Growing up in Elizabethan Times* (Batsford, 1980)

Cowie, Leonard, *Age of Drake* (Wayland, 1972)

Fines, John, *Tudor People* (Batsford, 1977)

Fox, Levi, *Shakespearean England* (Wayland, 1972)

Hart, R. W., *Battle of the Spanish Armada* (Wayland, 1973)

Hart, R. W., *Witchcraft* (Wayland, 1971)

Jones, Madeline, *Finding out about Tudor and Stuart Towns* (Batsford, 1982)

Kendall, A., *Elizabeth I* (Wayland)

Lane, Peter, *Elizabethan England* (Batsford, 1981)

Pringle, Roger, (Ed.), *A Portrait of Elizabeth I* (Ward Lock)

Taylor, Duncan, *The Elizabethan Age* Dobson)

Unstead, R. J., *Living in the Elizabethan Court* (A&C Black, 1975)

Zamoyska, Betka, *Queen Elizabeth I* (Longland, 1981)

Index

Picture Acknowledgements

The illustrations in this book were supplied by: courtesy of the Ashmolean Museum 20; BBC Hulton Picture Library 41 (top); courtesy of the Trustees of the British Museum 6; John R. Freeman (Photographers) & Co. Ltd. 10, 17, 53; Mansell Collection 13; National Monuments Record 32; National Portrait Gallery 4, 14, 16, 24. The remaining photographs are from the Wayland Picture Library.